READING POWER

High-Tech Vehicles

The Space Shuttle

William Amato

The Rosen Publishing Group's
PowerKids Press™
New York

Published in 2002 by The Rosen Publishing Group, Inc.
29 East 21st Street, New York, NY 10010

First Edition

Book Design: Christopher Logan

Photo Credits: Cover, pp. 5–6, 8–11, 13, 15 (top) © Kennedy Space Center; p. 7 © Charles E. Rotkin/Corbis; pp. 14–21 © NASA

Amato, William.
The space shuttle / William Amato.
    p. cm. — (High-tech vehicles)
Includes bibliographical references and index.
ISBN 0-8239-6007-2 (library binding)
1. Space shuttles—United States—Juvenile literature. [1. Space shuttles. 2. Space shuttles.] I. Title.
TL795.515 .A43 2001
629.44'1—dc21
                                            2001000273

Manufactured in the United States of America

Contents

The Space Shuttle   4

Going into Space   8

The Crew   14

Working in Space   16

Returning to Earth   20

Glossary   22

Resources   23

Index   24

Word Count   24

Note   24

The Space Shuttle

The space shuttle is a high-tech vehicle. It is used to take people and cargo into space. A space shuttle is made to be used more than 100 times.

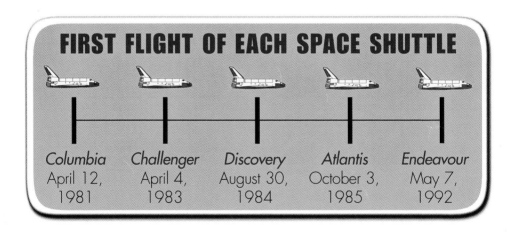

FIRST FLIGHT OF EACH SPACE SHUTTLE

Columbia	Challenger	Discovery	Atlantis	Endeavour
April 12,	April 4,	August 30,	October 3,	May 7,
1981	1983	1984	1985	1992

The space shuttle has three main parts. They are the orbiter, the fuel tank, and the rocket boosters.

Fuel Tank

Rocket Boosters

Orbiter

What's Taller?

The fuel tank on the space shuttle is taller than the Statue of Liberty.

154 ft.

151 ft.

Going into Space

The space shuttle is put on a large platform. The platform then moves to the launch site.

IT'S A FACT!

The shuttle weighs more than 4,500,000 pounds at liftoff. Much of this weight is fuel.

The space shuttle lifts off like a rocket ship. It takes only eight and one-half minutes for the shuttle to travel 200 miles from Earth. At 200 miles from Earth, the shuttle travels 17,500 miles an hour.

IT'S A FACT!

The rocket boosters can be used again. They fall to Earth after liftoff. Parachutes help them land safely.

The fuel tank supplies the shuttle with fuel at liftoff. The rocket boosters give the shuttle extra power for liftoff.

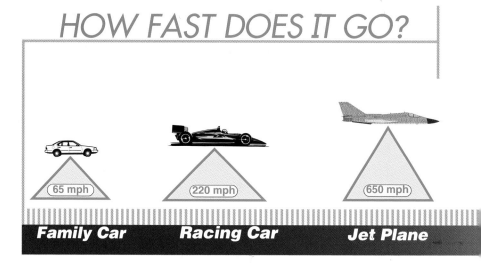

HOW FAST DOES IT GO?

65 mph

220 mph

650 mph

Family Car   **Racing Car**   **Jet Plane**

17,500 mph

Space Shuttle

The Crew

There are usually five to seven astronauts on each shuttle flight. Each astronaut must wear a space suit during liftoff.

IT'S A FACT!

Astronauts put on comfortable clothes after the shuttle is in orbit. All the clothes are fireproof.

The space suits keep astronauts safe. Special crews help the astronauts get dressed.

Working in Space

Computers help the astronauts run the space shuttle.

Astronauts also can steer the shuttle by hand. The computers help them know where to go.

Astronauts often go outside the shuttle to do important work. This is called a space walk.

This astronaut holds on to the shuttle's robotic arm to work on the space station.

This astronaut is fixing a satellite. Satellites help people on Earth get information.

Returning to Earth

After their mission, the astronauts return to Earth. The shuttle has wheels like an airplane has to help it land safely.

The mission is a success. The astronauts are proud of their work in space.

The shuttle has a parachute to help it slow down.

Discovery

Glossary

astronaut (**as**-truh-nawt) a person who travels into space

cargo (**kar**-goh) supplies carried by the space shuttle

fuel tank (**fyoo**-uhl **tank**) a large container for holding the fuel that powers the shuttle during liftoff

launch (**lawnch**) to move quickly off the ground

mission (**mihsh**-uhn) an errand or task that people are sent somewhere to do

orbiter (**or**-bih-tuhr) the part of the space shuttle that goes back and forth between Earth and space

rocket boosters (**rahk**-iht **boo**-stuhrz) rockets that help the shuttle lift off from the launch pad

space shuttle (**spays shuht**-l) a reusable spacecraft that carries people and cargo between Earth and space

space suit (**spays soot**) a suit that protects people in space

Resources

Books

Space Shuttle (Fast Forward Series)
by Mark Bergin and David Salariya
Franklin Watts (1999)

Look Inside Cross-Sections: Space
by Moira Butterfield, Nick Lipscombe,
and Gary Biggin
Dorling Kindersley (1994)

Web Site

NASA Human Space Flight
http://spaceflight.nasa.gov/

Index

A
astronaut, 14–21

C
cargo, 4
computers, 16–17

F
fuel tank, 6–7, 12

L
launch, 8

M
mission, 20–21

O
orbiter, 6

R
rocket boosters, 6, 10, 12

S
satellite, 19
shuttle, 4, 6–10, 12–14, 16–18, 20–21
space suit, 14–15
Statue of Liberty, 7

Word Count: 279

Note to Librarians, Teachers, and Parents

If reading is a challenge, Reading Power is a solution! Reading Power is perfect for readers who want high-interest subject matter at an accessible reading level. These fact-filled, photo-illustrated books are designed for readers who want straightforward vocabulary, engaging topics, and a manageable reading experience. With clear picture/text correspondence, leveled Reading Power books put the reader in charge. Now readers have the power to get the information they want and the skills they need in a user-friendly format.